Where Do I Fit In?

Stories by Leon Rosselson

Illustrations by Andy Hammond,
Blair Sayer and Anne Wilson

Contents

No Fair is Not Fair 2

Two of Each 23

Dreaming of Home 42

NO FAIR IS NOT FAIR

The visit was a disaster. It was hate at first sight.

Adam and Rob eyed the girls as though they were aliens. They spent the whole visit playing computer games.

The girls ignored the boys and listened to music on their headphones. They didn't bother to ask Adam and Rob if they wanted to listen.

Afterwards, Mum sat her boys down and attempted to explain.

"Look, it's definitely going to be a major change, but I'm sure in time you'll get along with the girls just fine."

"No, we won't," said Adam sullenly. He was a couple of years older than Rob.

"Well, you're going to have to get used to it," Mum declared, because I'm marrying their dad."

"We don't mind you marrying him. And we're prepared for him to live here," Adam told her. "We just object to those girls coming too."

"Where else are they supposed to go?" asked Mum.

Adam thought for a minute. "An orphanage?" he suggested.

"They're not orphans," said Mum. "What's the problem with them living here?"

Adam and Rob both started moaning at once. They didn't want to share a room ... the house would be too crowded ... the girls would spend ages in the bathroom ... Did they need to go on?

"Calm down," said Mum. "It'll be fine. We're all going to live together as one large family. You'll see."

"But we're perfectly all right as we are," Adam said.

"Don't forget," Mum added, "Emma and Nicole have lost their mum. They've had a hard time."

"What did she die of?" Rob asked.

"Cancer," said Mum.

"Farid's dad had cancer," said Adam.
"But he didn't die."

"Are you going to be their mum now?" Rob asked.

"I'll be their stepmum," Mum explained. "And I'll look after them, just like I look after you two."

"So is their dad going to be our dad?" asked Rob.

"Well, yes. Stepdad anyway."

"We've already got a dad," Adam pointed out.

"You have," replied Mum. "But he no longer lives here. He's got a new family now. And you haven't seen him in ages."

"He's still our dad."

"So you'll have two dads," said Mum.

"Do we have to call our stepdad … Dad?" asked Rob.

"What would you like to call him?"

"Pig face?" Adam suggested.

"I think it's high time you two went to bed," said Mum. "We'll discuss it further tomorrow."

Adam was lying in his bed, staring up at the ceiling. Rob pushed open the door.

"What's up with you?" Adam asked.

"Nothing."

"So why aren't you asleep?"

"Can I sleep in here?" asked Rob.

Adam groaned. "No. You kick in your sleep."

"I'll sleep on the floor."

"Don't be stupid."

"I'll be sharing your room soon anyway," said Rob. "When those girls move in."

"Well they haven't arrived yet, have they? So you can sleep in your own room."

Rob began to cry.

"Oh, whatever's the matter with you?"

"Don't know," Rob sobbed.

Adam sighed. "Oh, come on then. Get in. But if you kick me, you're out."

Rob stopped crying and crept in the other end of his brother's bed. They lay there in silence, imagining how their lives would soon be completely altered.

"I'm not going to speak to them," Adam told Rob.

"Nor me," agreed Rob.

"Maybe I'll run away and find our dad," Adam said.

"I don't think he wants us to live with him," said Rob. "Anyway, I don't want to leave Mum."

"Well," said Adam, "I've got to do something." And he turned on his side and switched off the bedside lamp.

The next day, Mum and Adam helped Rob move his bed and clothes, toys and books into Adam's room. Adam took a long piece of string and laid it on the floor, dividing the room in two. Rob had the smaller part.

"Don't put any stuff in my half," Adam warned Rob.

"It's not fair!" Rob complained. "There's not enough room for all my things."

"It's not my fault," said Adam. "It's all because of those stupid girls."

"It's awful. Why is Mum doing it?" Rob asked.

Adam shrugged. "Love."

"What about us?" said Rob forlornly.

"She's going to have to love those girls now," Adam said. "So she may not have enough for everyone."

Mum spent Saturday morning cleaning Rob's old room.

"Brian's going to change this wallpaper," she said.

"Why?" asked Rob. "It's great."

"I suspect Emma and Nicole won't be happy with a football design," Mum told him.

Rob became tearful again. His mum gave him a hug. "Poor thing," she said. "Don't worry. You'll get used to it. It'll be fun. You'll see."

"No, it won't," said Adam.

"By the way," Mum said. "Brian says you can call him Brian."

The boys stared at her.

"He says it's preferable to Pig face."

On Friday, the day before the wedding, a van arrived with furniture for the girls' room. Brian drove up later. The boys watched while their mum helped carry boxes in.

"What's in there?" Rob asked.

"Clothes, books, CDs. Things like that," Brian told him.

"There'll be no room for us soon," commented Adam.

"Where's their telly?" Rob asked, as they watched Brian drive away.

"Sold it," said Mum. "Brian got rid of most of their stuff. He wanted a fresh start, he said."

"So we're going to have to share our telly, then?"

"That's right," Mum said. "Sharing is the name of the game."

"It gets worse," said Adam.

Emma, Nicole and their dad moved in on Saturday, after the wedding.

On Sunday morning, the war began.

First, it was the war of the bathroom.

Emma ran into the bathroom seconds before Adam. He waited a few minutes and then banged on the door. There was the sound of the shower running. Again he banged. Emma started singing loudly.

Adam returned to his room, furious.

"I knew this would happen," he told Rob. "She's doing it on purpose."

"You can use the bathroom before me if you like," Rob said.

"You don't understand anything!" shouted Adam.

There was a scampering sound on the landing. Adam rushed out. He was just in time to see Nicole rushing into the bathroom and Emma closing her bedroom door. He yelled out furiously and thumped the wall.

There was a race every morning after that. Rob didn't join in, but the other three began to get up earlier and earlier to be first in the bathroom.

After a week, their parents decided to put an end to the competition. Every Sunday, they pinned up a list. On it was written who could use the bathroom at what time and for how long. Everyone had to obey the list, or lose a week's pocket money.

Next was the war of the television.

The boys only had a short walk to school. The girls still went to their old school, a bus ride away. Adam and Rob nearly always arrived home first and chose the programmes they preferred to watch.

The boys were watching cartoons one afternoon when Emma and Nicole came in.

"There's a pop music programme on the other channel," Emma said. "Can we watch it?"

"No," said Adam. "There are more cartoons after this."

"That's not fair!" complained Emma. "You've been watching for ages and we never get a chance to choose."

"I don't mind if we watch pop music," said Rob.

"Yes, you do," said Adam. "You like cartoons."

"You're selfish, mean and horrible!" Emma said angrily. "I wish we hadn't moved here."

"So are you! And I wish you hadn't come here too!" shouted Adam

"Stop it! Stop it!" Nicole cried.

Emma tried to grab the remote control from Adam. The next minute, they were rolling around the floor, wrestling for the zapper. They bumped into tables and knocked over chairs until … CRASH! A vase was lying broken on the floor.

"Now look what you've done!" Rob shouted.

Nicole rushed out of the room, screaming, "You're all horrible!"

They were banned from watching television for a week. After that, they each got to choose one programme a day to watch.

Then came the war of the washing-up.

It was a rule that the children had to clear the table and wash up after Sunday dinner.

"I'll wash up this week," Adam said.

"You did it last week," said Emma. "It's my turn."

"I'm good at it."

"No, you're not! You leave food on the plates."

Adam shrugged. "OK, clever clogs. You wash, I'll dry."

"I'll put the things away," Rob said. "Nicole can help me."

Adam found a bit of potato on one of the plates. He scraped it off and threw it at Emma. It hit her on the ear.

"You're rubbish at washing-up!" he said scornfully.

Emma was washing a bowl which was full of water. She turned and threw it over Adam. He was soaked. He whipped Emma on the legs with his tea towel.

Nicole, seeing her sister attacked, picked up a ripe plum from the fruit bowl. She threw it at Adam and it splattered on his head.

"Hey, don't do that!" shouted Rob, and he grabbed a dirty dishcloth from the kitchen table and threw it at Nicole.

"Look what you've done! You've ruined my dress!" she wailed.

When their parents came in a few minutes later, the kitchen was a battlefield. The children were a mess. Their clothes were wet and stained. Bits of food and two broken plates lay on the sopping floor.

"OK, you're all grounded!" Mum shouted. "No pocket money. No television. No cinema. No outings. Nothing."

"For two weeks," Brian added.

"What about the fair next Sunday?" Adam pleaded. "You promised we could go."

"Grounded. Two weeks. Now clear up this mess!" shouted Brian.

After they'd cleared up, the four children went to the boys' room for peace talks.

"Two weeks!" exclaimed Adam. "Your father's too strict."

"He isn't usually," said Emma. "He's just following your mum."

"She's never strict," Adam said. "Well, only sometimes."

"Arguing isn't going to get us anywhere," Emma told them. "Maybe if we were nice to each other for the rest of the week, they'd change their minds."

"Mum doesn't change her mind," said Rob.

"Perhaps we should be nice to each other anyway," Nicole said.

"Why?" asked Adam.

"We just should."

"I don't mind being nice," said Rob.

"We could give it a go," Emma suggested. "We ought to stick together anyway. Against our parents."

"Down with parents!" Adam smiled.

"Well, we're sort of brothers and sisters now, aren't we?" added Emma.

"Sort of," Adam agreed. "OK. Let's try not to fight for the rest of the week."

So they tried.

Rob allowed Nicole to play with his games, and Nicole let Rob use her special box of paints. Adam showed Emma his computer games, and Emma taught Adam chess. She even let him win the odd game.

The next Sunday, their parents came down for breakfast to find all four children lined up in the kitchen.

Emma was holding a placard. On it was written:

"What's all this?" Mum enquired.

"It's a protest," Adam explained.

"I see," said Mum.

"We've behaved well all week," Adam said.

"So we think you should permit us to go to the fair," added Emma.

"I see. What do you think, Brian?"

"Well – maybe we were a little harsh," Brian said.

"If we let you go, will you carry on behaving well, and being civilised to one another?" Mum asked.

"Definitely."

"Of course."

"We're friends now."

"In that case," Mum said, "you're no longer grounded."

The children grinned. Adam let out a whoop of delight. "I'm going on the roller coaster!" he shouted.

"Bet you don't," said Emma. "You'll be too scared."

"You mean you'll be too scared," retorted Adam.

Their parents exchanged looks, and burst out laughing.

Two of Each

"Daniel," he heard his mother call. "Telephone."

"Who is it?" he asked.

"Your dad. He wants to talk to you."

Daniel shook his head. "I'm not in."

"Don't be silly." His mother pushed the phone into his hand and walked away.

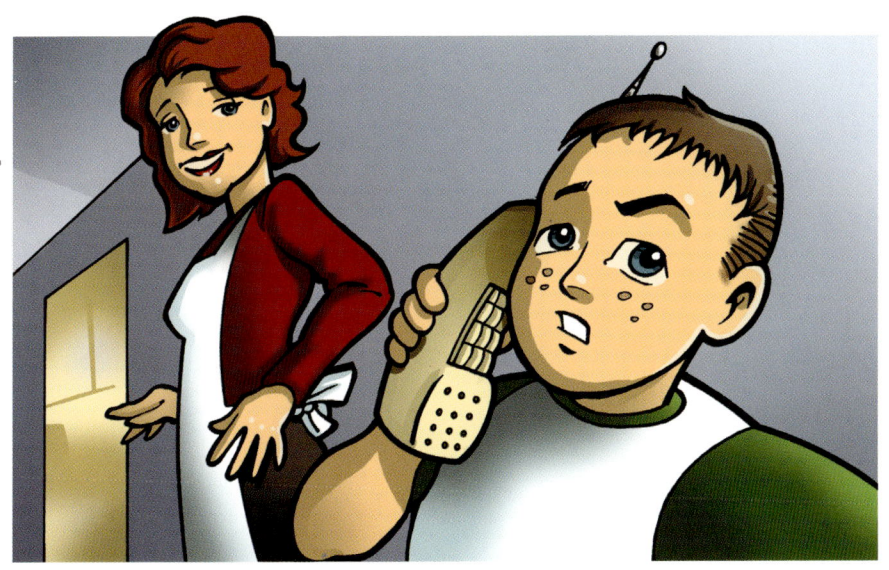

Daniel put the phone to his ear and listened.

"Daniel?" he heard his father say. "Are you there?"

"No," said Daniel.

"How are you, Daniel?"

"Fine."

Then came the usual questions: How are you doing at school? Are you being good for your mother? Any plans for the holidays? In reply, Daniel gave his usual one-word answers: Yes … No … OK … What did his father want from him?

Soon the conversation petered out.

"Maybe I'll come and see you in the holidays," his father said.

"OK."

"Maybe in a few weeks, if I can sort things out. We'll have a lot to talk about."

"OK."

"Bye, Daniel. Be good for your mother."

Daniel put the phone down and wandered into the kitchen where his mother was frying chips for their tea.

"What did your father have to say?" asked his mother.

"Nothing much."

"He must have said something."

"I don't remember."

His mother sighed. "I know it's hard for you. But he still loves you, you know. He's still your dad."

"Why did he leave then?"

"He wasn't abandoning you," his mother explained. "It was us. All we did was argue. Don't you remember?"

Daniel remembered lying in bed trying to block out the angry voices. He remembered the front door slamming and his mother sobbing. That was nearly a year ago. He hadn't seen his father since, only spoken to him on the telephone.

"What about the holidays?" his mother asked. "Is your dad taking you somewhere?"

"Who cares?" said Daniel. "I'd rather go on holiday with you."

His mother took the chips out of the bubbling fat. "Sorry, Daniel," she said. "I can't afford it this year."

"But we always go away in the summer!" Daniel cried.

"I know," said his mother. "But everything's different now. Money's tight. I'm sorry."

"It's not fair!" Daniel moaned. "All my friends are going somewhere. Pete's dad's taking him to Ireland on a fishing holiday."

"That's nice," his mother said. "Lay the table please, Daniel."

"Everyone's going away," said Daniel bitterly. "It'll be dead boring here."

"We can go on picnics," his mother suggested. "We could go on Sunday if the weather holds. Would you like that?"

"Where to?" asked Daniel.

"Down to the river. You could even swim if it's warm."

"I hate swimming."

"You used to enjoy it there."

Daniel hated being reminded of what he used to do.

"Anyway, we haven't got a car anymore," he said.

"We can go in Rory's car. Do you want a fried egg with your chips?"

Daniel nodded.

"Do you mind going with Rory?"

"I don't care."

"So, shall we go?"

"If you like."

Daniel wasn't keen. There'd be no one to play with and he didn't think Rory would be much fun. Not that he had anything against him. Rory was all right, except when he tried too hard to be chummy. Anyway, Rory was his mother's friend, not his.

Sunday was sunny, and Rory came to meet them. Daniel's mother had prepared a picnic basket.

"You ready then, Danny boy?" said Rory, grinning.

"My name's not Danny boy," Daniel mumbled to himself. "I'm never called that."

"What about your swimming trunks, Daniel?" his mother asked.

"I told you. I hate swimming."

"Take them anyway. You might change your mind."

He groaned but threw his trunks and a towel into his bag, along with a ball and his cricket bat. Maybe he'd find some other boys there he could play with. Otherwise it would be a complete bore.

Daniel squeezed himself into a corner of the back seat, trying to make himself invisible, while his mother and Rory chatted in the front. From time to time, Rory would glance back at him and say, "How're you doing, Danny boy?" and Daniel would grunt.

They turned off the motorway and drove down the country lanes that led to the river. Daniel gazed out of the window, remembering other car journeys with his parents when they'd played I Spy and sang songs in loud voices.

From the car park, it was a short walk to the river. Already, people were sprawled on the grassy bank, toasting themselves in the sun. Small children paddled in the river and built mud walls. There seemed to be no children of Daniel's age.

"It's going to be a hot one," said Rory.

Daniel's mother looked at the cloudless sky. "Perfect," she smiled.

The three of them walked along the bank, hunting for a good spot. They found a place and parked their bags and towels.

Rory began rubbing suntan cream on his arms and legs. Daniel put suntan cream on too.

Rory jumped up and grabbed Daniel's cricket bat. "Who's for a game of cricket?" he sang out.

Daniel got to his feet unwillingly, and threw the ball at Rory's legs. But Rory blocked it with the bat.

"Come on, Angie," said Rory. "On your feet. No slacking!"

Angie? Angela was his mother's name. Sometimes his father called her Angel for a joke, but never Angie. Why did Rory have to call her that?

His mother laughed and stood up. "Come on, Daniel. We'll soon get him out."

Daniel threw the ball again. Rory struck it hard. Daniel, jumping to his right, caught it one-handed.

"Good catch for a young un," said Rory, handing him the bat.

For about an hour they played. Despite himself, Daniel found that he was enjoying the fun. His mother entered into the spirit of the game, happily running for the ball and laughing when she missed a catch. Daniel hadn't heard her laugh like that in a long time.

At last, she collapsed breathless on the grass, panting, "That's enough for me."

"Me, too," said Rory. "Must be getting old."

Daniel was left standing there, holding the ball. He looked at the two of them together. He had the feeling he didn't belong there.

He walked down to the river and stared at the sunlight gleaming on the water. When he turned back, he saw that his mother was talking to Rory. They didn't appear to be bothered about him.

He started to walk along the river bank.

His mother's voice caught up with him. "Where are you going, Daniel?"

So she had noticed him after all.

"For a walk," he shouted back.

Daniel followed the river away from the crowds. Fishermen stood patiently holding their rods, boxes of wriggling maggots beside them.

Further on, there was a natural swimming pool. This was the spot they had come to on bright summer Sundays, when they were a proper family. This was where Daniel had learnt to swim. Even though he'd been frightened, he'd kept on trying. He smiled as he remembered how proud his father had been.

A group of boys were in the pool, diving and swimming, laughing and splashing. Daniel felt annoyed that they were there. It was a special place for him and his father. Why did they have to be there?

If only his father hadn't gone to Scotland. He could have come on the picnic instead of Rory. His father would have spent time with him, taken him fishing maybe. Daniel pictured his father fishing by the river, wearing the green jersey and funny green hat he always wore on holiday …

Suddenly, the boys were out of the water and heading towards him. It was too late to run. Five boys, with mocking expressions on their faces, surrounded him. Daniel tried to stop trembling. He didn't want them to know that he was afraid.

"Fancy a swim?" the biggest boy said.
Daniel shook his head.
"You look hot with all those clothes on."
"You look like you need to cool down," said another boy.

Before Daniel could move, they were on him. He struggled and cried out. But no one came to his rescue.

Two boys held his arms and two held his legs as they lifted him into the air and swung him backwards and forwards.

"One ... two ... three ..."

Daniel flew through the air and hit the water. He felt the water fill his eyes, his ears, his mouth. He was choking ... He was drowning ...

In a panic, he pushed himself to the surface and gulped in air, coughing and spluttering. Somehow he managed to splash his way to the bank.

Gasping for breath and shaking with fear, he rubbed his eyes. Everything was blurred.

Again, he felt hands grasping his arms and legs. Again, he felt himself being swung backwards and forwards.

Then a voice commanded, "Put him down!"

"What's it got to do with you?" asked one of the boys.

"Put him down. Look at you – five big lads picking on one smaller un."

"Are you his dad?"

"That's right. Put him down."

Daniel felt himself being lowered onto the grass.

"We were only fooling about," said one of the boys.

Daniel heard the sound of laughter, then running, and boys jumping into the water. He breathed a sigh of relief. When his eyes finally cleared, he saw Rory bending over him.

"Are you OK?" asked Rory.

Daniel struggled to his feet. "You're not my dad!" he said.

"I know I'm not," said Rory. "But your dad isn't here, is he?"

Water dripped off Daniel's clothes and water squelched in his trainers. He was shivering.

"Come on," said Rory. "We'd better get you back."

They started to jog, but Daniel's sopping trainers and socks felt so uncomfortable that he took them off and carried them.

"Your mum's going to have a fit," Rory said.

"Don't tell her," said Daniel.

"What?"

"Don't tell Mum about those boys throwing me in. And you saving me."

"Why not?"

"You don't have to tell her. She'll fuss. I'll say I fell in."

"OK, Danny. If that's what you want."

"I'm Daniel. Not Danny."

Rory grimaced. "Right," he said. "Sorry. I forgot."

"Are you going to marry my mum?" Daniel asked.

Rory laughed. "That's jumping the gun," he said. "Would you mind if I did?"

Daniel shrugged.

"I'd make her happy," said Rory. "I promise."

Daniel's mum was sitting up, looking anxious. "Daniel!" she shouted. "What on earth happened?"

"I fell in the river."

"How did you manage that?"

"It was easy," said Daniel.

"Well, you'd better take those wet clothes off and put your swimming trunks on. Lucky we brought them. Spread your clothes out in the sun. They might dry out before we go home."

They had their picnic and played another game of cricket. Then Daniel lay back and dozed while Rory told a long, complicated story about how he'd once been attacked by a bear in Canada.

By the end of the afternoon, Daniel's clothes were dry enough to put back on.

"I reckon that was a pretty good day," Rory said, as they walked back to the car.

"I haven't enjoyed myself that much in ages," said Daniel's mother.

"How about you, Daniel?" Rory asked.

"Falling in the river was fun," replied Daniel.

Rory drove them home.

When they got back, there was a message for Daniel on the answer machine. "Ring your dad for some good news," it said.

He dialled the number and waited.

Then he heard his father's voice.

"Hi, Dad," replied Daniel.

"Hi, Daniel," said his father. "Listen. I've managed to get two weeks off work. How would you like to come to Scotland for a holiday? I thought we might go on a fishing trip."

Daniel's heart leapt. "OK," he said.

"Moira's looking forward to meeting you."

There was a silence.

"Daniel?"

"Yes, Dad. Great."

"Good. I'll phone next week and arrange the details with your mother."

"What's the good news?" his mother asked, when Daniel had put the phone down.

"Dad's taking me on a fishing trip."

"That's wonderful."

Daniel pulled a face. "With Moira."

"Oh, well. You'll have to meet her some time."

"Rory wants to marry you," said Daniel.

His mother's face went pink. "Daniel!"

"It's all right," Daniel told her. "I don't mind."

"Come here," said his mother, and she gave him a big hug.

"Two of each!" Daniel exclaimed.

"What?"

"Two mums and two dads."

His mother smiled. "Aren't you the lucky one."

"I expect I'll get used to it," said Daniel.

Dreaming of Home

Everything is different now. Everything I once had is now gone. My country. My father. My big sister. They are all gone. All I have left is my mother. My poor mother.

My name is Yasmin. I cling to my name. I say it over and over again, because I'm frightened that if I don't, I might forget who I am.

Let me tell you my story. At least, let me tell you what I can remember.

I remember my big sister, grinding corn to make bread. I can still see her outside our hut, holding a long pole and pounding the maize. Up and down went the pole, over and over again. The bangle on her arm slid up and down. This is the first thing I can remember.

42

I also remember being frightened. Explosions. Shouting. Screaming. The war had come to our village. The huts were on fire. The earth was on fire. Everyone in the village was running.

Hunger. I remember hunger and thirst. Days in the hot sun with nothing to eat. Walking. Being carried. My throat on fire. My body aching.

Then confusion. There were soldiers. Who were they fighting? Why were they fighting? I didn't understand.

The next thing I remember is a camp outside the city. At last we had some food. Rice and bits of goat meat. My father and my big sister were not there. The soldiers took them, my mother said. So now I was the big sister. I was the only sister.

In the camp, there was nothing to do. The boys played football. I watched them all day long, kicking the ball. Only it wasn't a real ball. It was a bunch of crumpled up paper held together with string.

I remember holding my mother's hand, and watching the sun make sparkling diamonds on the sea as the big ships sailed into port. We had never seen the sea before. It seemed to make my mother happy. Perhaps she was dreaming of flying far away across the water.

But what I remember most is the terrible day we walked into the city to see the market stalls.

People crowded the streets. The women wore brightly-coloured cotton dresses. The sunlight bounced off the white walls of the buildings, dazzling my eyes. I was dancing along beside my mother.

Suddenly, everything exploded. Terror scattered the crowds. Stalls were overturned. I heard gunfire. There was an explosion so loud it seemed to be inside my head.

A building near us collapsed into rubble. Everything seemed to be happening in slow motion. I was screaming, but I couldn't hear my screams. There was a swirl of dust and a truck roared into the road behind us. It was crammed with men firing guns.

The next minute, I was lying in the street and blood was oozing out of my arm. My mother pulled me to my feet. We ran and ran, sobbing and screaming, until we were back at the camp.

You don't believe me? You think I am making it up? Sometimes I wonder myself. Was it really like that? Is that how it happened?

The wound wasn't bad, and my arm soon healed. Then we were running again, running from the war that was exploding in the city.

I don't know how many days we kept on walking. Sometimes we rode in lorries. We lived on rice and goat's milk, until eventually we crossed the border into Kenya. We found a camp where we could rest and have some peace.

It was then that my mother made up her mind. She wanted me to have a different life. A better life. Other people wanted to go back when the fighting stopped. But my mother said, "No." She was going to take me to England. But how could we go anywhere with no money?

If you believe in something enough, if you really want something, it will come true. That's what my mother used to tell me.

And it did come true. We were able to fly to England. I'm not sure how it happened. I know my mother sold her gold bracelet. And other villagers helped, some a little, some more.

So, one bright and sunny morning, we flew up into the blue sky. I closed my eyes and clung to my mother. I was terrified.

When I opened my eyes, I could see nothing but sky.

"Goodbye, my country. Goodbye, Somalia. Will I ever see you again?"

Arriving at the airport in England made me feel stupid. I couldn't understand what was happening, or what anyone was saying. I wanted to go home, but I didn't have a home anymore. I held my mum's hand as we followed people along endless corridors, until we found ourselves in a long queue.

The next thing I remember is being in a small room. A man asked my mum questions which, of course, she didn't understand. She took a piece of paper from her bag and handed it to him. It had a name and a number on it. I think it was the name of someone who helped Somalis when they arrived in England.

The man took the paper and went away. We sat there waiting. A woman came in with a drink for me, a sort of sweet fizzy juice which tasted funny, some biscuits with chocolate on, and a cup of tea for my mother. That was our first English food.

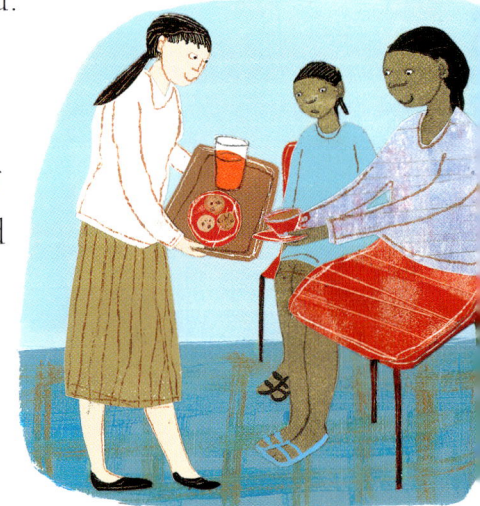

We waited and waited. In the end, I was so exhausted, I went to sleep on the chair. When I woke up, there was a different man in the room and he was speaking Somali with my mother. We were going to ask for asylum. That's what my mother explained to me.

My first days in England were like a nightmare. I was in a daze.

Before we left the airport, they took our fingerprints and photos. I don't know why.

I couldn't make sense of anything. I didn't know what we were doing, or where they were taking us. I was frightened all the time. I thought everyone was staring at me because I was different.

First of all, I was freezing. It was supposed to be summer, but even when we saw the sun, it didn't warm us up, and we had no warm clothes. I didn't understand how anyone could live in such a cold country.

Then there were all the cars and buses in the streets. I couldn't believe how many there were. Such a smelly place. No animals though. No camels, goats or sheep. I missed the animals.

And it never got properly dark at night. There were always lights and street lamps. In Somalia, you can see millions of stars at night, but in London, you can only see the lights of aeroplanes flying overhead.

They took us to a kind of hotel where other refugees were staying. It was dingy and cold, and the paint on the ceiling was flaking off. My mum and I slept in the same bed – which was good, because we kept each other warm.

We couldn't cook for ourselves, so we had to eat whatever food we were given. The first morning at breakfast, I looked at the curly orange bits in the bowl and wondered what they were – and how I was supposed to eat them.

My breakfast at home was a big pancake-shaped bread, sprinkled with sugar.

Of course, I'm used to the food now. I quite like some of it. But some things I'll never get used to. Fish fingers, for a start.

When they gave us fish fingers in the hotel, I looked at them suspiciously and prodded them with my fork. My mum just pushed her plate away. When another refugee explained what they were, and what they were called in English, I laughed so much I nearly fell off my chair. Fish fingers? Do fish in England have fingers?

It was better when they moved us into a hostel. We shared a kitchen with other refugees, and we could do our own cooking and shopping.

At first, shopping was awful. We didn't understand English money, and we never had enough money to buy what we wanted.

After a few weeks, I became quite good at adding up English money. But my mum couldn't get the hang of it. She grew very worried when we queued in the supermarket, in case we'd got more than we could pay for.

I didn't worry anymore about what people thought of us. The only time I got upset was when we passed some footballs and I asked my mum to buy me one. She shouted at me and said the money wasn't for buying footballs.

Just after that, my mother stopped being strong.

All the time, from the very beginning when war had driven us from our village, she'd been strong and brave and protected me and comforted me. Whatever happened, I knew she'd be there to help me.

When we first came to England, I relied on her to hug me and hold my hand, and tell me that everything would be all right. At night especially, she helped me sleep, telling me stories and singing me songs – making me feel safe.

Suddenly, she stopped being strong. She spent hours of the day in bed, staring at the wallpaper. What was she looking at? What was she thinking?

She wouldn't tell me what was wrong. She wouldn't say much at all. She wasn't eating properly either. She relied on me more and more to do the shopping and the cooking.

When I started going to school and learning English, I thought my mum would be pleased. I used to come back and tell her how we had books at school, and paper to write on, and pictures on the walls – all the things we didn't have in Somalia. I told her I didn't feel so much of an outsider anymore.

But she didn't seem interested. She was fading away. My strong mother was fading away, becoming a ghost. What was I to do?

On my way to school, I passed a row of shops. I loved to look in the shop windows at all the things on display. I'd dream of how one day, I'd buy everything I wanted. I couldn't believe there were so many different things in the world.

The shop I liked best had all sorts of funny objects in the window – pictures, boxes, vases, plates, photo frames, beads, ornaments, cushions. I loved looking at them, but I didn't dare go inside.

One day, coming back from school, I stopped at the shop and noticed a picture in the window that I hadn't seen before.

It was a beautiful painting of the seaside. The sun was shining in the clear blue sky, birds were flying overhead, and the waves with the sunlight on them looked real. Standing at the water's edge, staring out to sea, were two people. It could have been a mum and her daughter. It could have been my mum and me.

I decided that I had to have the painting. I would take it back to our room and hang it on the wall. My poor ghost of a mother, instead of staring at the wallpaper, would look at it and remember good things, and grow strong and be my mum again.

I know it sounds crazy, but I was sure that this picture was the magic that would save my mum from fading away. But where would I get the money to buy it?

I pushed open the door of the shop and went in. I was trembling. The man sitting by the cash register looked at me in surprise. He was tall and quite old and had a friendly face.

"Hello there," he said. "What can I do for you?"

"My name's Yasmin," I told him.

"That's a nice name. Are you looking for something, Yasmin?"

"How much is the picture?" I asked.

"Which picture?"

"The one in the window," I replied. "The sea picture."

"Ah, yes. That one. Dreaming of Home?"

"Sometimes," I muttered.

"That's the name of the painting," he said. He went to the window and looked at the label. "Fifty-five pounds."

My heart sank. Fifty-five pounds! It would take me for ever to save all that money.

"I'm sorry," he said, as he saw the disappointment on my face.

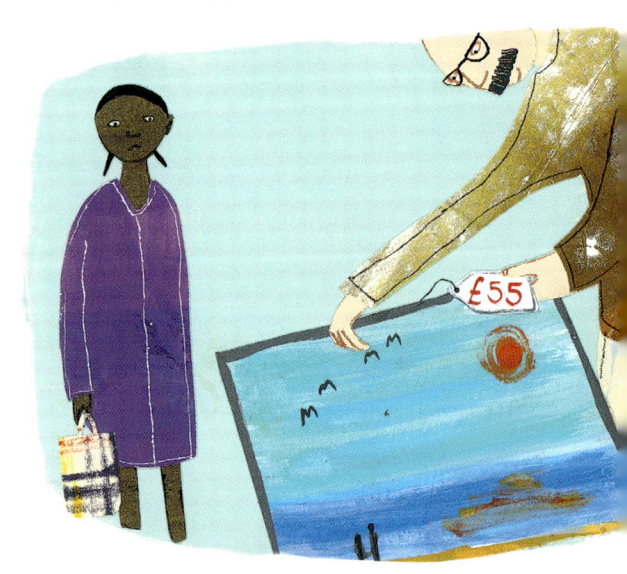

My mum seemed worse when I got back. She looked sad and thin, and even more ghost-like. I tried to cheer her up by telling her what I'd done at school.
She just nodded and went on staring at nothing.

I dreamt of the painting that night. I dreamt it was hanging on the wall, and when my mum saw it, she clapped and laughed and began dancing around. But when I woke in the morning, there was nothing on the wall but dirty wallpaper.

The next day, walking back from school, I stopped again at the shop with the seaside painting. The picture wasn't in the window. Had somebody bought it?

Anxiously, I pushed open the door and went in. The man wasn't there. I could hear him rummaging around at the back of the shop. The painting was leaning against a wall.

Now, I know what I did next was wrong. I promise you that I didn't mean to steal it. I just wanted to borrow it, so that my mum could see it and be happy again. I meant to bring it back, really I did.

I picked up the picture and was about to walk out of the door when the man came back. He strode over to me and grabbed my arm.

"What's all this about, young lady?" he said sternly.

My heart was thumping. My mouth was dry. I couldn't speak.

"Where do you think you're going with that?" he asked.

"My mum," I whispered.

"You can't just take things that don't belong to you. Don't you know that?"

I nodded.

"Your mum?" he said. "Well, let's see what she's got to say about this."

He took the picture and led me out of the shop, locking the door behind him. Where was he taking me? Were we going to the police station? What would my mum say when she knew I'd been arrested as a thief? It would kill her.

"Come on, young lady," he said. "You're going home."

"I haven't got a home," I said.

"Where do you live?"

"In a room."

"That's where we're going then," he said.

I was shaking with fear all the way back to the hostel.

Up the steps into the hostel we went. Up the stairs we climbed, and into the room where my mother was sitting on the bed, staring as usual. When she saw me, with the man gripping my arm, she looked panic-stricken.

"I believe this is your daughter," the man said, freeing my arm. "I'm afraid she's been a very naughty girl."

I don't know whether my mother understood what he was saying, but she understood that I was in trouble. She rushed over to me and pulled me to her, shouting in Somali, "No! No! You can't take her! She's all I have left!"

The next moment, she was holding her hands up to the heavens and weeping and wailing and sobbing. The man must have thought she'd gone mad.

"Hoyo!" I said. "Mum. It's all right. I'm not a thief. I only meant to borrow it. Please."

Then I realised. She wasn't just weeping for me. She was weeping for my father and my big sister. She was weeping for her village and her people, and for everything she'd lost. I burst into tears too, and we held each other and cried and cried, until we could cry no more.

When I looked around for the man, he'd gone. The picture was propped up against the wall. There was a note next to it. It said:

You can keep the painting for one week. Please bring it back safely.

"Look, Mum," I said. "Look at the painting!" I held it up for her to see. "Isn't it beautiful? It's called Dreaming of Home."

She gazed at it wonderingly. Then she looked at me, and for the first time since she'd come to England, she smiled her old smile. I knew then that it was going to be all right. I knew then that she was going to be my brave, strong mother again.

And she was.